Mountain Biking
CHECK IT OUT!

Kristin Eck

The Rosen Publishing Group's
PowerKids Press ™
New York

1

SAFETY GEAR, INCLUDING HELMETS, KNEE PADS, GLOVES, SHIN GUARDS, AND ELBOW PADS SHOULD BE WORN WHILE MOUNTAIN BIKING. DO NOT ATTEMPT TRICKS WITHOUT PROPER GEAR, INSTRUCTION, AND SUPERVISION.

For Mike

Published in 2001 by The Rosen Publishing Group, Inc.
29 East 21st Street, New York, NY 10010

First Edition

Book Design: Michael de Guzman
Layout: Emily Muschinske, Nick Sciacca

Photo Credits: p. 5 © Cheyenne Rouse; p. 7 © Hank de Vre/Mountain Stock; pp. 9, 13 © Brian Bahr/Allsport USA; p. 11 © Elsa Hasch; p.15 © CORBIS TempSport; p. 17 © Tony Donaldson; p. 19 © Mike Powell/Allsport USA; p. 21 © Agence Vandystadt.

Eck, Kristin.
    Mountain biking : check it out! / Kristin Eck.
       p. cm.— (Reading power) (Extreme sports)
    Includes bibliographical references and index.
    Summary: Simple text introduces mountain biking, discussing equipment, terrain, and competition.
    ISBN 0-8239-5698-9
    1. All terrain cycling—Juvenile literature. [1. All terrain cycling.] I. Title. II-III. Series.
2000
796.6'3—dc21

Manufactured in the United States of America

Contents

You can ride a mountain bike in the water. You can ride a mountain bike in lots of places.

A mountain bike has thick tires. These tires let you ride over dirt and bumps.

A mountain biker needs a helmet, gloves, and special glasses.

Mountain bikers race.
Mountain bikers race
to see who can go
the fastest.

This mountain biker rides up a hill on a dirt path.

Some mountain bikers ride in the woods. It is called free-riding when mountain bikers ride in the woods.

Some mountain bikers ride on the snow.

Some mountain bikers ride on dirt roads. They go fast. They make clouds of dust.

Mountain biking is a sport in the Olympics! Mountain bikers win medals. Would you like to be a mountain biker?

21

Glossary

dirt (DURT) Mud, dust, or soil.

helmet (HEL-mit) What a biker wears to keep his or her head safe.

medals (MED-ulz) Awards or honors given to people who have won, or achieved, something.

Olympics (oh-LIM-piks) World sports competition.

race (RAYS) To compete to see who can go the fastest.

tires (TY-urz) Hoops of iron or rubber around the wheels of a bike or machine.

Here is another good book to read about mountain biking:

The Fantastic Book of Mountain Biking
by Brant Richards
Catherine Ward (illustrator)
Rob Shone (Illustrator)
Copper Beech Books (1998)

To learn more about mountain biking, check out this Web site:
http://www.usacycling.org

Index

Word Count: 128

Note to Librarians, Teachers, and Parents

If reading is a challenge, Reading Power is a solution! Reading Power is perfect for readers who want high-interest subject matter at an accessible reading level. These fact-filled, photo-illustrated books are designed for readers who want straightforward vocabulary, engaging topics, and a manageable reading experience. With clear picture/text correspondence, leveled Reading Power books put the reader in charge. Now readers have the power to get the information they want and the skills they need in a user-friendly format.